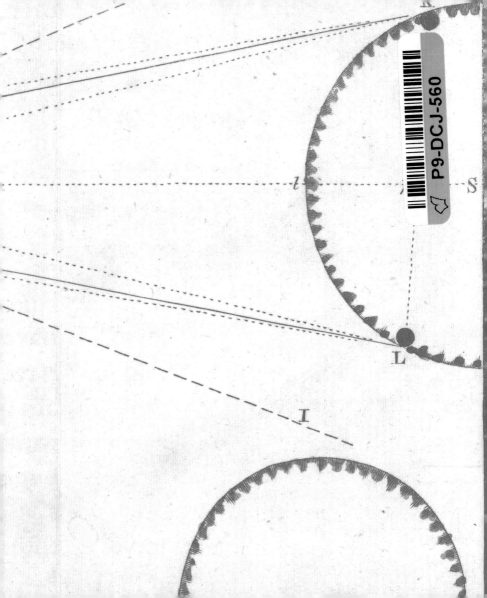

CHICKEN, SHADOW, MOON & more

BOOKS BY MARK STRAND

POETRY

Blizzard of One   1998

Dark Harbor   1993

Reasons for Moving, Darker, & The Sargentville Notebook   1992

The Continuous Life   1990

Selected Poems   1980

The Late Hour   1978

The Story of Our Lives   1973

Darker   1970

Reasons for Moving   1968

Sleeping with One Eye Open   1964

PROSE

The Weather of Words   2000

Mr. and Mrs. Baby   1985

The Monument   1978

TRANSLATIONS

Travelling in the Family   1986
(poems by Carlos Drummond de Andrade, with Thomas Colchie)

The Owl's Insomnia   1973
(Poems by Rafael Alberti)

ART BOOKS

Edward Hopper   1993

William Bailey   1987

Art of the Real   1983

FOR CHILDREN

Rembrandt Takes a Walk   1986

The Night Book   1985

The Planet of Lost Things   1982

ANTHOLOGIES

The Golden Ecco Anthology   1994

Best American Poetry
(with David Lehman)   1991

Another Republic
(with Charles Simic)   1976

New Poetry of Mexico
(with Octavio Paz)   1970

The Contemporary American Poets
1969

Mark Strand

CHICKEN, SHADOW, MOON & more

TURTLE POINT PRESS
New York   2000

811
Strand

Library of Congress Cataloging-in-Publication Data:

Strand, Mark, 1934–
     Chicken, shadow, moon and more / Mark Strand
  -- 1st ed.
     p. cm.
     LCCN: 99-71393
     ISBN: 1-885983-45-x

     I. Title

   PS3569.T69C45 2000   811'.54
                       QBI99-1580

Printed in Hong Kong

Front cover: Mark Strand, *Collage,* 1999
Text and cover design and composition by Anne Galperin

Contents

C O N T E N T S *continued*

To John and Adele

Mark Strand

CHICKEN, SHADOW, MOON & more

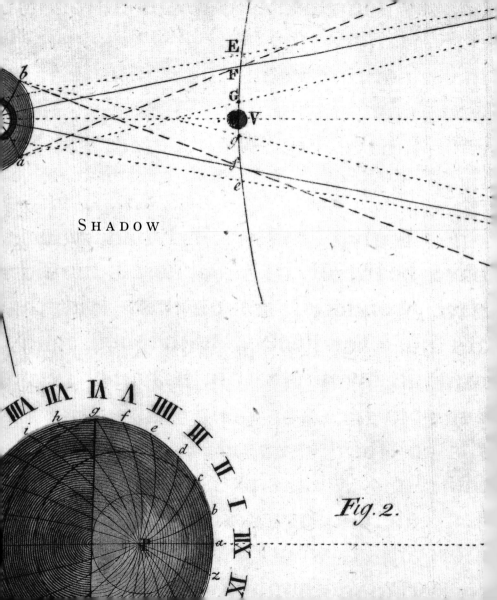

E
F
G
V
g
f
e
b
a

SHADOW

VIII VII VI V IIII III II I IX X
i *h* *g* *f* *e* *d* *c* *b* *a* *z*

Fig. 2.

The shadow of Naples

The shadow of stanzas waiting

The shadow of daylight is absence

The shadow of a mother includes another

The shadow of chaos is order

The shadow of the hawk is the robin

The piano's shadow is a cape

The cape's shadow is a woman

The shadow of one dream is another dream

The shadow within a dream is infinite

The shadow of a boat is an anchor

The shadow of regret is tragedy

The shadow of love is loss

Oh my! The shadow is back and is waiting

The shadow of paint is only paint

The shadow of rain is wetness unto itself

The shadow of morning is lean

Come back, shadow of my youth

Shadow me, and tell me where I've been

Come back, warm shadows of the Sundays of my youth

Even the brightest poem is haunted by shadows
The shadow of the mother, the shadow of the father
Shadows are robes the sun keeps dropping
Come back, lost shadows, syllables of midnight
To plead for a shadow is to plead for mercy

PARADISE

The lunatic paradise of clouds

The buried paradise of old utopias

The plentiful paradise of russet potatoes

The glassy paradise of unbroken sleep

The French paradise of Brasil

The echo's paradise of itself diminished

The wind in paradise is more like a scent

The guitar in paradise is too big to be played

A sick man's paradise looks like a landscape by Puvis

Rage in paradise is like a steam pipe bursting

Fred Astaire is still on a stairway to paradise

The forms of paradise are drawn from memory

The sighs of paradise are like the sighs on earth

The feel of paradise is like the touch of an August night
in mid-February

The custodians of paradise were once artists

The toys of paradise wind themselves

The mirrors of paradise reflect only one face

Dinner in paradise tastes like dessert but is made of lamb

Oblivion in paradise is a passing thought

Greetings in paradise sound like farewells

People in paradise love to wear black

The rivers of paradise are not really wet

Paradise is a secondary necessity

Pain in paradise is perfect and much sought after

In paradise the flushing of toilets is a sad reminder

The poor in paradise have smaller wings

In paradise lightning is a flash of song in paradise

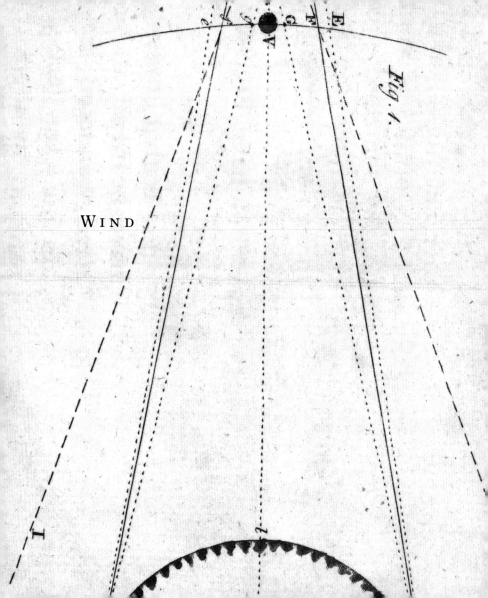

The dream wind of prophecy

The mortal wind of hospital corridors

The impossible wind that lives in the tomato

The glistening wind that riffles the sea

The disordered wind of naked speech

The white wind of the Himalayas

The middle wind of concession

The monotonous wind of stones

The dark wind of stars

God bless the banjo's wind

God bless Baudelaire's wind of the wings of madness

And the wind of the ant in his labors

The accessible wind of storms

The whirling wind within the kiss

The wind of the west gathering steam at sea

A fast wind leaves a blue trail

A tropical wind sleeps in the palm

A boreal wind lounges on glaciers

The wind in the wake of a rushing woman is a gown

The wind of the onion leaves a trail of tears

The wind that leaves the earth will never come back
The wind that roars is only practicing
God bless the green wind of poetry
God bless the humming wind of happiness
God bless the meaningless wind of circles

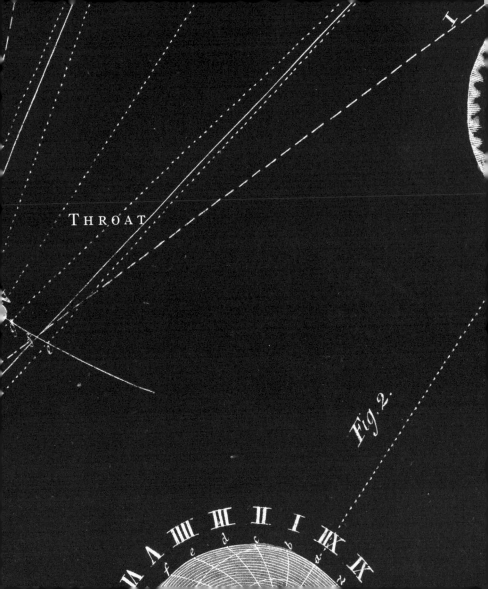

THROAT

Fig. 2

Ⅷ Ⅶ Ⅵ Ⅴ Ⅳ Ⅲ Ⅱ Ⅰ Ⅻ Ⅺ Ⅹ

The throat is the history of what has been said

The throat shows only one movie: "The Tongue"

The throats of angels are lined with gold

The throat's favorite food is sausage

A lover's throat is a vase of flowers

A sore throat is often the end of speech

Grass will not grow in a throat

Hair does well in a criminal's throat

The throats of Egyptian cats are like sleep

The moon's light in a throat is like salt on a melon

The people of Philadelphia have short throats

The people of Baltimore have teeny throats

The people of Atlanta hardly have throats at all

The planet of throats is still undiscovered

The flag of the throat is covered with ants

The throat likes food, but only in passing

In earliest times the throat lived apart from the body

Can a throat ever be left outside

Doctor, look at my throat and say what you see

The throat has no scenery worth talking about

Back at the ranch we have at least fifty throats

There was a bronze cast of the poet's throat in Central Park

We stared up at the throat and snow began falling

Only his powerful ears outdid his throat

Bronze ears in the park, bronze throat in the middle

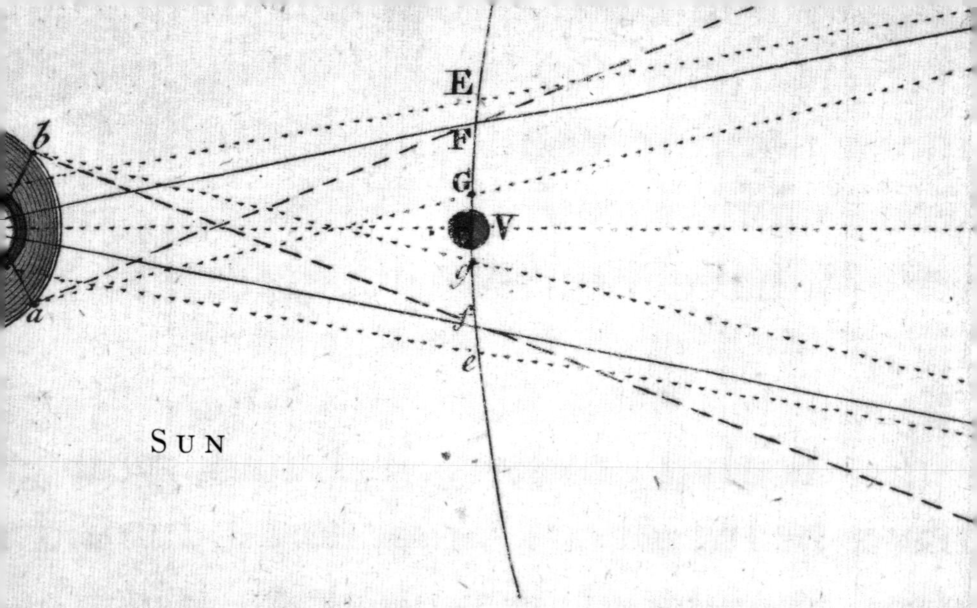

E
F
G
V
g
f
e

b
a

SUN

VIII VII VI V IIII III II I XII XI X IX

i h g f e d c b a P z

Fig. 2.

The meditations of the sun are lost in space
The palace walls are covered with sun
The sun throws down a ladder of light
The sun is an eye that sees too much
The sun lives in endless day, that is, until it dies
The sun is a kind of music not yet heard
The sun is the sun of its parts
Inside the sun is a room full of ashes
The sun shines so the moon can read
The sun counts for nothing in the milky way
The sun has vermillion cousins

The life of the sun depends on candles

The sun is the night's pornographer

Even angels fear the sun's reprisals

The sun's pomp is all myth

The sun hardly ever made the headlines

We can wait all day for the sun to go down

Hurry, Harold, the sun is faint

Hurry, Henry, the sun needs paint

Water the sun and you get burned

Cover my losses, the sun is looking

When the sun is high bees go wild

The sun just happened the way we did

The sun's catastrophes were overstated

Blow into the sun and become red in the face

What are feelings without the sun

What is the sun without sleep

The sun is blond by day, brunette by night

I remember a bowl of sunlight in Rome

How I loved that bowl of sunlight

The cold red of the Arctic sun is upon me

Slow down, my sun, and sit here for a while

For I am done when the sun is done

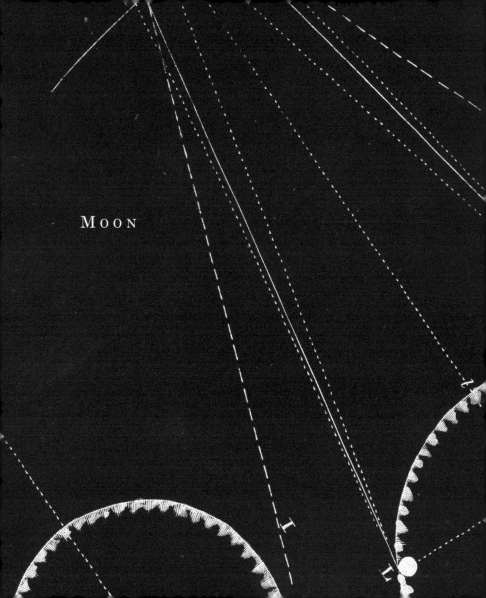

The man in the moon is a rabbit in Mexico

The moon is the sun's forgotten child

A fire on the moon is never visible

The moon aches for the visit of birds

The sleep of the moon ends in darkness

The moon is the eye of the scholar

The moon sideways is still the moon

The moon shivers in the winter sky

The wings of the moon were tossed overboard

The politician of the moon—how sad!

Empty the moon and empty your heart

The moon is a stone that floats

The moon wears a hood so it can sleep

Once upon a time the moon had legs

Piero della Francesca was born on the moon

A peacock lives on the moon when it can

The moon's horses have only three legs

The moon's pillows have all turned to stone

Oh, if the moon could speak it would only say "Oh"

Money is junk on the moon

Mormons dream of more moons

A woman in bed with the moon weeps a lot

The museum of the moon is badly lit

The moon carries itself lightly

If the moon fell, it would miss the earth but only by inches

Beware the bearded secretaries of the moon

In a million years the moon will sing

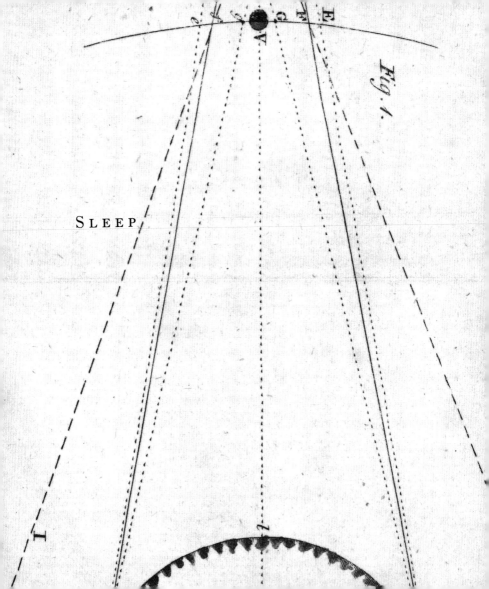

SLEEP

The sleep of the foot inside the shoe
The sleep of the shoe in the dark of the closet
The sleep of the sun before it rises
The sea sleeps at the side of the shore
The moon sleeps with its eyes open
Leaves sleep in the arms of mystery
A cloud will sleep within itself
The sleep of light is invisible
The sleep of meaning within a word
The sleep of madness inside of reason

The sleep of money inside the pocket

The lemon weeping for lack of sleep

The sleep of the future within the clock

The shadow cast by a star in the sleep of another star

The sleep of nakedness within desire

The sleep of desire in the flight of bees

February sleeps while June walks back and forth

The tired sleep of too much sleep

The sleep of the genius in her studio

The fluorescent sleep of a horse in the Peruvian midnight

The drummers have come, but they are noiseless—
> someone must be asleep

When an ant falls from a building, it thinks it's asleep

The grass of sleep covers the bones of the true

Sleep is always asleep

When sleep awakes, it forgets what it was

The knowledge of sleep is the knowledge of nothing

Sleep is a hole inside of the night

HOUR

I

Fig. 2.

IX I II III IIII V VI

The extra hour given back to eternity

The hour gained by travelling west

The hour of the imagined empire

The deepest hour of the darkest sea

The guilty hour that precedes catastrophe

The hour that it takes to go from here to there

The haunted hour of the knowledge of death

The hour in which the moon darkens

The hour that moves through the mind like cloudshadow

The blue hour that rests on the roof of the house

The hour that is the mother of minutes and grandmother of seconds

The swollen hour of pain, enough, enough

The hour when mice run in the walls

The bronze hour of electrical weather

The cloistered hour of the nun's great moment

The necklace of hours the widow wears

The numbing hours of a night in Nome

The sound of hours in the breathing of plants

The central hour that exists without you

The hour in which the universe begins to die

The hallucinatory hour that hangs forever

The hour of excess that equals two hours of self-examination

The hour that flashed on the skin

The hour of final music

The hour of painless solitude

The hour of moonlight upon her body

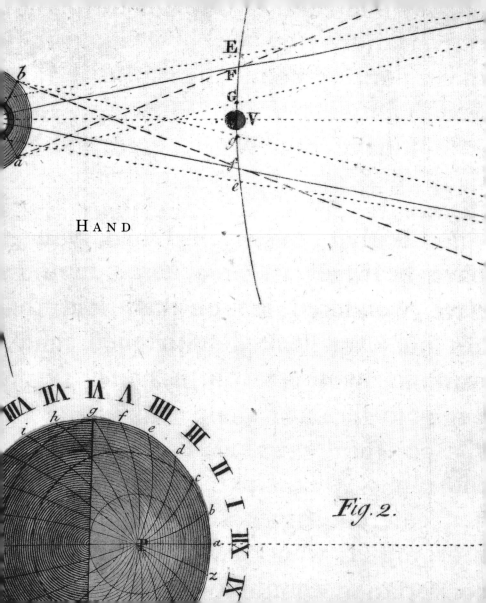

HAND

Fig.2.

The tempestuous hand of Carmen Miranda

The glass hand breaking on the kitchen floor

The hand that becomes a dog's head on the wall

A hard left hand, then a right, and another right

The hand that holds the house of cards

The hand that weighs nothing

The hand a snake wishes it had

The hand of the last man waving goodbye

His other hand hanging, the hand without bones

The cold hand of snow on the hillside

The hand of sleep just waking up
The small hand at the end of the huge arm
The hand that turns blue only in Zurich
The hand that's a glove for another hand
The diamond studded casket for the missing hand
The hand that pushes trucks across the carpet
The hand that is given without being asked for
The hand of the milkman, growing large
The hand floating down from the clouds
The hand of nothingness reaching for something

The folded hands that wait in the wings

The golden hands of Benvenuto Cellini

The savage hand of excitement

The spent hand of melancholy

The hand that hands this to you

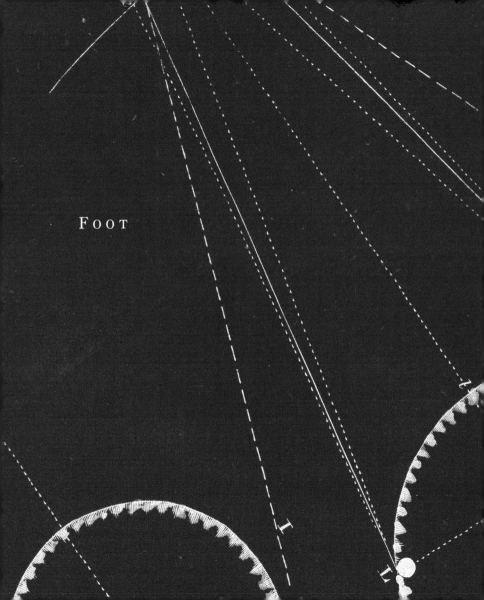

FOOT

The shapeless foot of a stranger that toys with the mind

The elegaic foot of the moon in a bed of parsley

The lapis foot in a mob of toes

The charismatic foot that rattles when it moves

The angelic foot that gathers no moss

The foot with fingers is loathed by the leg

The foot of The Great One had a toy mother

The foot of The Great One casts a blue shadow

Every foot says Go, every hand says Stay

The top of the foot slopes moonward

The tragic foot of the beauty parlor

The eternal foot of the observatory

The fleeting foot of the hydro-electric plant

The foot that sings so long for now and much love

The foot with bones that crack like cane

Kissing the foot is like learning a language

The foot came apart when you said No

What the foot wants is a sweater

There's a foot in the closet of the setting sun

Trust me, the foot will come home before dark

Loving the foot means loving a heel

The foot wishes it was more like a swan

The foot sets its heart on the limits of wonder

What the foot knows about hair would fill a book

The foot a foot away from being one of your feet

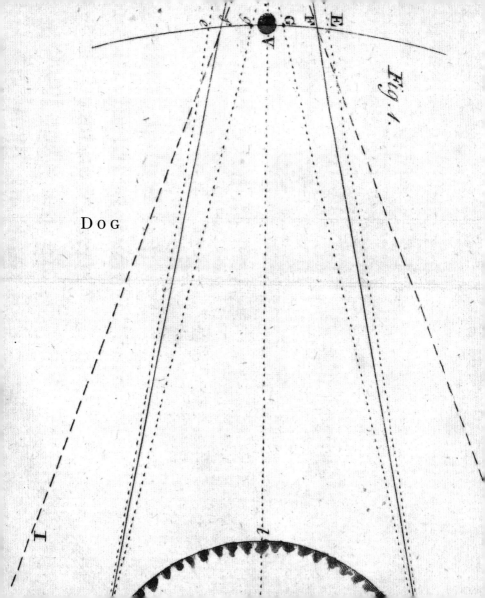

Fig. 1.

Dog

A dog is human just like the rest of us

A dog is someone with a bone in his mouth

A dog can wag his tail the way we do

Look at that dog pee on the bush

That dog has moved on to the next

A dog can love more than a dog

A dog in a skirt is ready to dance

A dog has names for himself that a man can't know

A dog gets lonely at the drop of a hat

A dog struggles against infinity

A dog's emptiness is a fullness elsewhere

Come here, my dog, my love, and sit with me

When my dog stares at me, I fall to my knees

I weep when my dog barks commands

If my dog loves me, I am happy

A dog is a barber's nightmare

A dog is a silent witness

If a waitress kisses a dog she's open-minded

When a dog is boss, everyone struts

When a dog wants sex, everyone howls and scampers around

Sometimes a leg is enough for a dog

I know a dog for whom China is nothing

I know a dog whose paws are hands

A dog is smarter than you can imagine

A dog doesn't go into the office

A dog licks the hand that feeds him

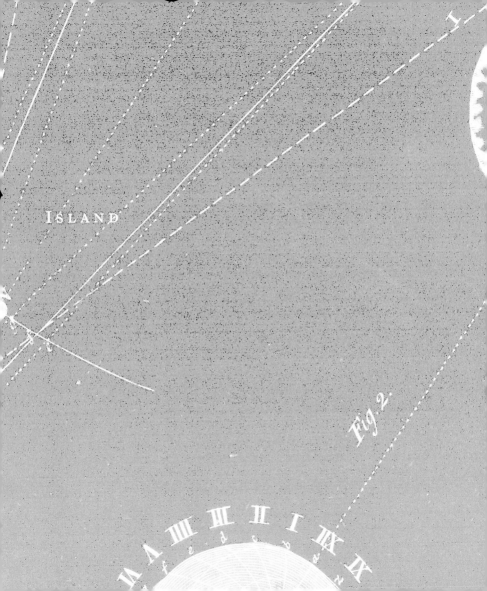

ISLAND

Fig. 2

VI V IV III II I XII XI X IX

The island of the weeping bush

The island of relinquishment

The island of green pangs

The island of blue villages

The island of aching amorists

The island of golden tedium

The island of shrinking trees

The island of serene sides

The island of congenial fruit

The island of mambo-dancing widows

The island of pale speech

The island of massive membranes

The island of monster turkeys

The island of dirty music

The island of maidens blowing saxophones

The island of moon thieves

The island of Spaniards prophesizing

The island of glittering darkness

The island of humming llamas

The island of pink turtles

The island of chocolate monkeys

The island of exiled grief

The island of ghost promenades

The island of dancing undertakers

The island with nothing on

The island of erotic rhetoric

The island of vice presidents

The island of false weather

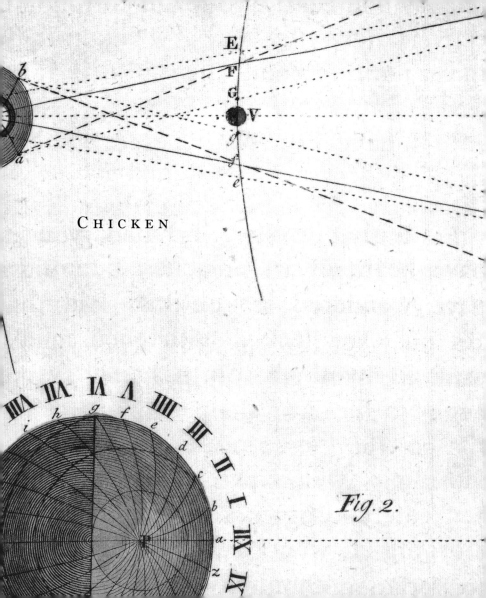

CHICKEN

Fig.2.

Long live the chicken with its head

A carefree chicken is not a chicken

That big chicken is a flood of feathers

The fragrance of chickens is an excess of chicken

Come back, my chicken, my rose

The sacred chickens of Egypt will not be forgotten

My bashful chicken does not cluck

When Phoebe doth behold the chicken coop, she wants to cry

Oh, faint primrose beds where chickens want to lie

A musical chicken is a beautiful thing

A tortured chicken in its sleep will howl

What's another chicken to Asclepius

The imperial chickens of Rome have turned into cats

Chickens have an instant nature

O the immaculate passion of chickens

Modest chickens never crow

If a chicken answers the door, you're at the wrong party

A twisted chicken will always check in

The global chicken warms its egg

The egg blows up and kills the chicken

The cosmic chicken is a lesson to us all

The poetry of chickens is without imagination

If a chicken wore clothes, we couldn't eat it

I ate five small chickens all in one sitting

If a goose is available, why choose a chicken

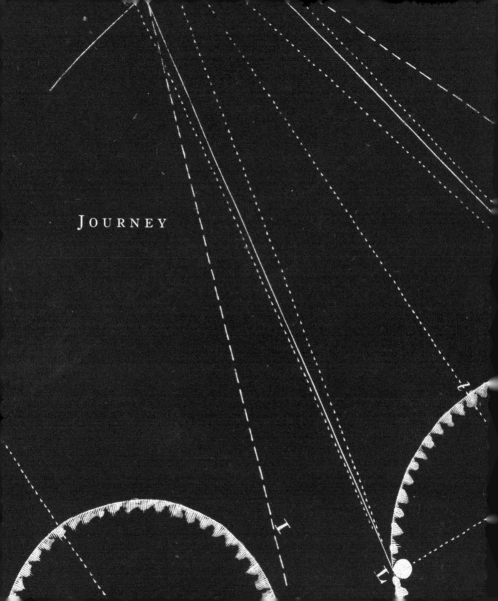

JOURNEY

A journey continues until it stops
A journey that stops is no longer a journey
A journey loses things on its way
A journey passes through things, things pass through it
When a journey is over, it loses itself to a place
When a journey remembers, it begins a journal
Which is a new journey about an old journey
A journey over time is different from a journey into time
An actual journey is into the future
A reflective journey is into the past

A journey to Rome is both

A journey to Pittsburgh is probably neither

A man on a journey keeps waving goodbye

A crystalline journey is frozen in time

A journey tests its own limits

A celestial journey ends in heartache

The arm is a journey within the sleeve

An empty journey forms a circle

A journey without an umbrella is incomplete

A journey always begins in a place called Here

Pack your bags and imagine your journey

Unpack your bags and imagine your journey is done

A journey is one step too many

A journey with fog must be a pastel

If you're afraid of a journey, don't buy shoes

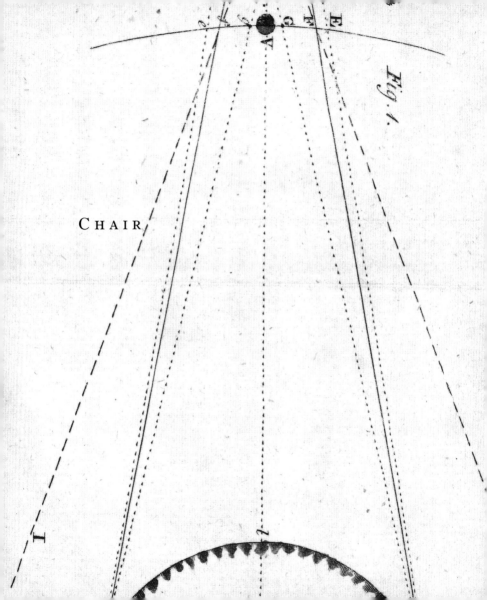

CHAIR

Fig. 1.

An easy chair is a comfort to all

The shape of a chair is wrong over time

A chair in Alaska sinking down in summer ice

A chair far off in a field at sunset

A chair lost among the machines of the sea

The stubborn chair in a world where everyone stands

The chair that will bear the weight of a genius

The bottomless chair of Bottom's dream

A chair with three legs cannot be trusted

All chairs have fire in their future

But a marble chair will be forever

They sat upon a chair and wished upon a cloud

The secret wish of a chair is to be a horse

And yet, if a chair had arms it would play the viola

What a comfort a chair in the kitchen can be

The sculptor thought he made a giraffe; it was a chair

A chair is the ultimate defense against chaos

A chair on top of the tree is a home for clouds

A nude in a glass chair is a little like champagne

Musical chairs is not a game but a delusion

A hundred chairs make no sound at all

A chair lives somewhere outside the body

A chair's secret is not to breathe

A chair carved of a carrot can be eaten

No one expects a chair to smile

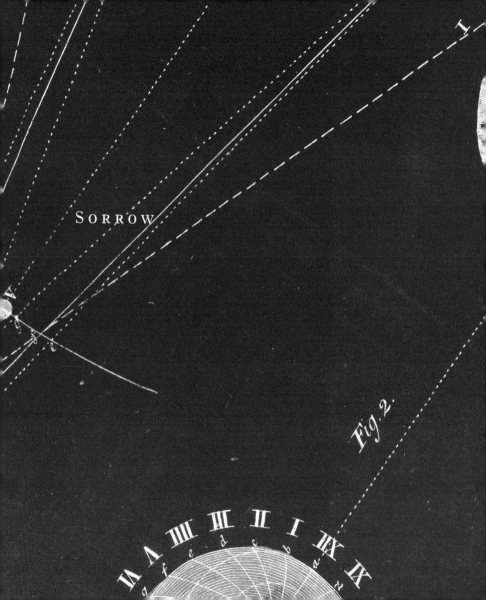

SORROW

Fig. 2.

In the hotels of sorrow the guests weep continually

In the shops of sorrow nothing is right and everything costs
        too much

On the streets of sorrow even the children wear black

In the airports of sorrow all flights are cancelled

In the houses of sorrow no one admits to sorrow

The pastures of sorrow are filled with discarded appliances

The days of sorrow are shadowy and deep

The graveyards of sorrow are happy but empty places

Oh where is the sorrow of sorrows

Say there will never be sorrow greater than this

Parties are such sweet sorrow

Sorrow is the soul's candy

Sorrow can be bought, but it's usually free

The mole and the bat are companions of sorrow

There's the mysterious sorrow of ants with nothing to do

The lovers of sorrow will settle for more of a bad thing

The good old days of sorrow were even worse

A perfect sorrow is almost sorrow

The snows of sorrow just keep falling

The Sorrows are a dance team from Tintern Abbey
The Sorrows hate dancing, which is why they dance
Many sorrows begin with an Easter egg hunt
Other sorrows begin with a swimming pool incident
A song begins when sorrow comes aknockin'

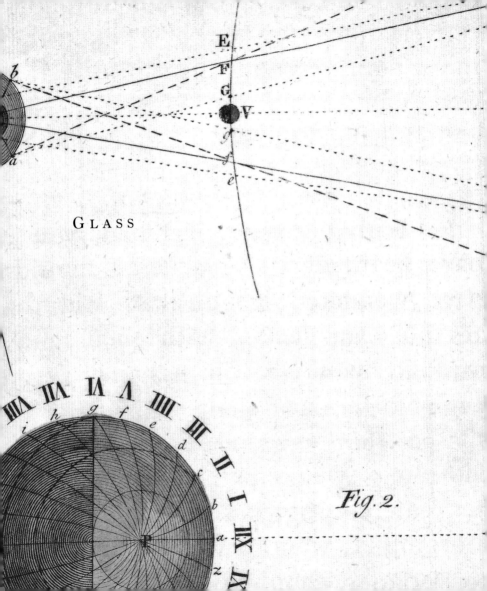

GLASS

Fig. 2.

A glass face doesn't need a mirror

But a looking glass sees nothing

A glass flag needs a stiff breeze

A glass book with invisible writing is hard to find

People who live in glass houses want to be seen

They will be seen without glasses

Glass mittens on a cold day will fool Jack Frost

Leaves of glass tinkle in the wind

A sleeper dreams and his glass pillow fills with smoke

Nothing is more elegant than a man with glass hands

The enigma of a glassy stare

The watery smile of glass teeth

A glass umbrella is a window to the rain

People in Iceland wear glass slippers

A glass clock listens to time

A glass lip can bite itself

Glass underwear for the exhibitionist

On a still day the sea is glass

A glass flower has no scent

A glass repeats itself to no purpose

Glass cookies with raisins make a stunning dessert

An empty glass is nakedness inverted

A symphony of bananas beating on glass

At the end of the village nothing but glass

A glass mountain and a glass sky cannot be told apart

A glass thought makes a pure sound

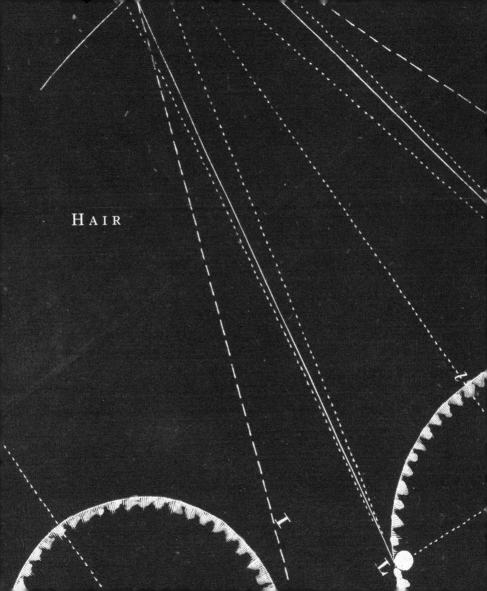

HAIR

It is hard to see into a house filled with hair

Lots of hair on a small person looks worse than one hair
       on a big person

It could be that hairy women like hanging out with hairy men

Lick a cat and get a hair ball

When hair starts to grow in your yard, get the big razor ready

Hair in an ice cube will ruin a drink

Oh the bushes and braids of the hair parade

Nobody looks for great hair in a painting

The stylists of hair prefer to wear hoods

When a couple has a falling out, they lose their hair

You can say she has beautiful hair

You can't say she has beautiful hairs

When you raise your voice, you let down your hair

When you weave the sunlight in your hair, you enact a poem

The mystery of hair will never be solved

When Moses crossed the Red Sea, he was parting somebody's hair

Dolores, let down your hair and grieve with me

If men had more hair, they'd walk on all fours

Come sit by my side and bring your hair with you

Hair doesn't grow on buldings—never has
Suppose birds had hair and mammals had feathers
Would Charlotte Rampling's eyes be the same without her hair
Oh the hair of Charlotte Rampling
A night in July, your hair, and you

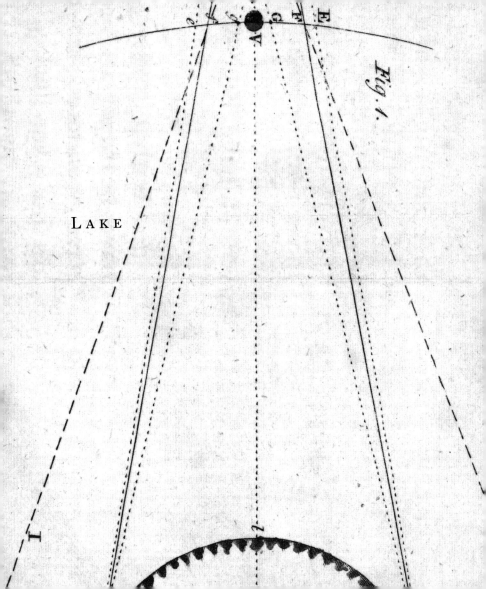

To drowse away the summer on a lake

To feel the limitations of the lake

To count the lake's two colors

To feel that something is wrong with the lake

I really like the lake, said the woman next door

You push a lake out of the way, but it comes right back

A lake could mean the end of chaos

A lake swallows itself every night

I like this lake, too, I said to the woman next door

There once was a lake with only one wave

Fifty young men were staring into the lake

If you speak to the lake, you must ask yourself why

To test the true material of the lake

To dip the oars of sleep into the surface of the lake

To feel the lake give birth to words for itself

A lake could fall into the wrong hands

Even an artificial lake needs real water

Oh the lake is beautiful, and meaningless, and I love it

What lake is that you're talking about

No lake at all—I'm bad at remembering lakes

Is it the way a lake looks or how it feels that matters
In that respect a lake is like a chair
The lake was full of stars, the moon, the tops of trees
Someone was playing a trombone across the lake
On this side of the lake a silence was building up

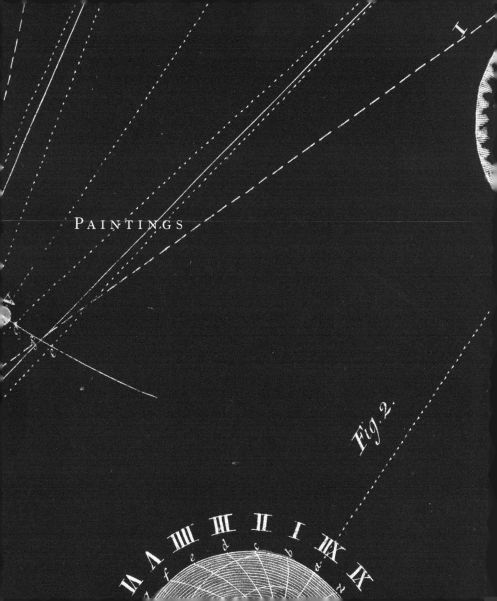

PAINTINGS

The paintings of A were of rock piles

The paintings of B were influenced by A

The paintings of C were of miracles flattened

The paintings of D were of cruise ships on fire

The paintings of E captured a lost transparence

The paintings of F contained a number of frozen animals

The paintings of G seemed always larger at night

The paintings of H announced the approach of the unreachable

The paintings of I completed themselves endlessly

The paintings of J stood in relation to nothing

The paintings of K were like parties under water
The paintings of L acknowledged the power of chance
The paintings of M offered readings of sunrise and smoke
The paintings of N left nothing to the imagination
The paintings of O contained elements of emptiness
The paintings of P were of babies swimming
The paintings of Q were of nudes having lunch
The paintings of R foretold the coming of midnight
The paintings of S seemed to shrink as they were looked at
The paintings of T were conceived in unison

The paintings of U referred to the Age of Vegetables
The paintings of V concealed their humble origins
The paintings of W hastened the end of self-portraiture
The paintings of X suggested a fury of something-or-other
The paintings of Y couldn't be looked at without music
The paintings of Z died of neglect the minute they were shown

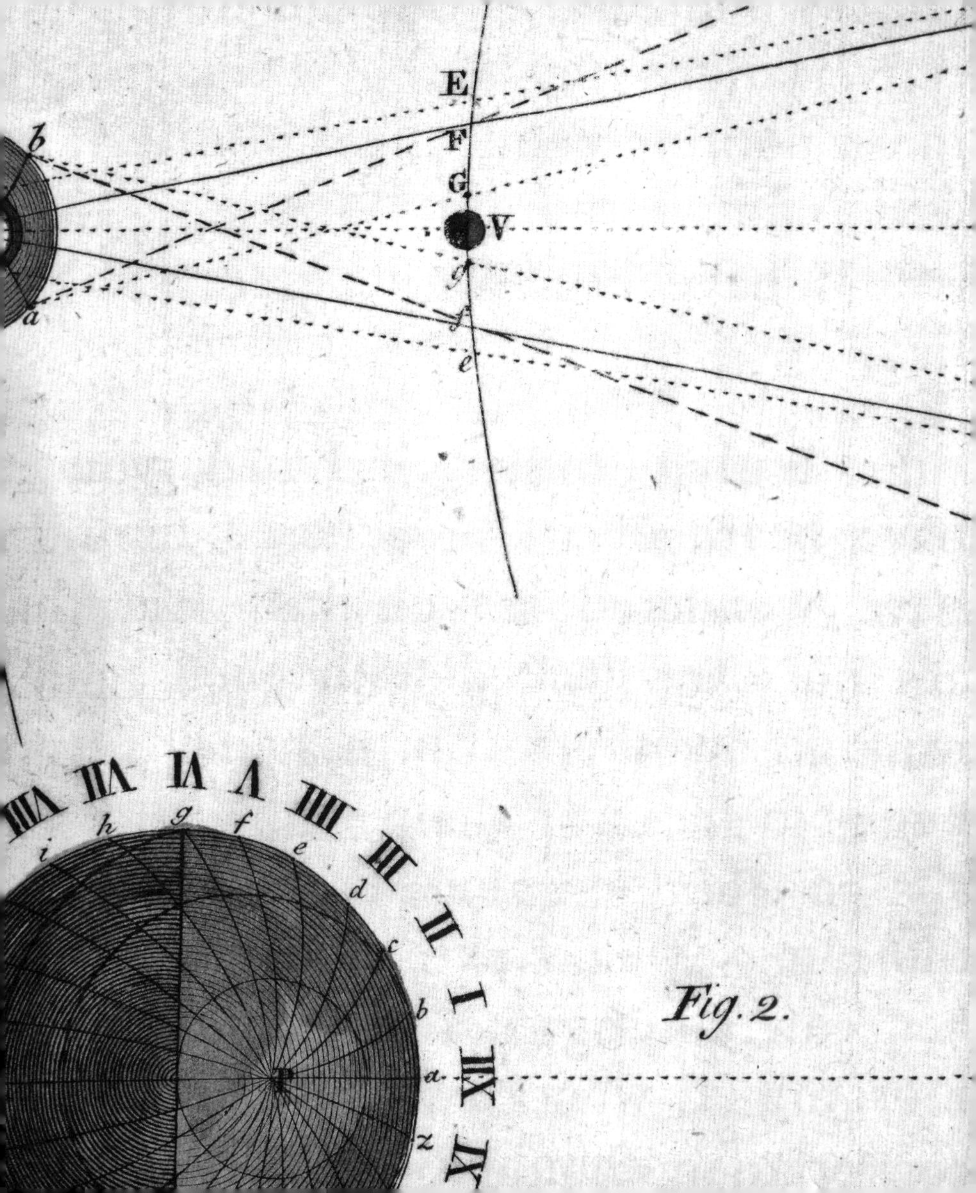

Fig.2.

A NOTE ABOUT THE AUTHOR

Mark Strand was born in Summerside, Prince Edward Island, Canada, and was raised and educated in the United States. He is the author of nine earlier books of poems. He is also the author of a book of stories, *Mr and Mrs. Baby,* several volumes of translations (Rafael Alberti and Carlos Drummond de Andrade among them), a number of anthologies and two monographs on contemporary artists (William Bailey and Edward Hopper). He has received many honors and grants for his poems, including a MacArthur Fellowship, and in 1990 he was chosen as Poet Laureate of the United States. In 1999 he received the Pulitzer Prize for *Blizzard of One*. He teaches in The Committee on Social Thought at The University of Chicago.